Too Much Yet Not Enough

Jadzia Avyanna Stevens

TOO MUCH YET NOT ENOUGH

iUniverse books may be ordered through booksellers or by contacting:

iUniverse
1663 Liberty Drive
Bloomington, IN 47403
www.iuniverse.com
844-349-9409

ISBN: 978-1-6632-1786-8 (sc)
ISBN: 978-1-6632-1787-5 (e)

Library of Congress Control Number: 2021901872

Print information available on the last page.

iUniverse rev. date: 01/29/2021

My poems always meant the world in a single word. As I loved more, hurt more, and cried more, all I had to offer creatively was released into tissues, in my car on the way home from any event, in the shower unable to clean off the stale feeling. Stale, was what I became. Fresh was what decade and now my words mean nothing.

Contents

Stars

Have you ever looked at the sky at night and thought

“I wonder how many stars there are?

How many stars does it take to light up the night sky?

How much smog does it take to cover
a billion dead sun's lament?"
How many times have aliens looked
at our planet and thought
"Eradicate the enemy, they have doomed their future.

They have killed their planet already."
How much poison have we inhaled?
How many breaths away are we from death?

How many people with the most beautiful eyes have cried?
How many times have we died
Before realizing that we are just ghosts following the same routine every day unaware because we are not at rest…

How many years before we stop chasing paper
with a currency that in full reality
Is not worth shit compared to the stars in the sky

That for now

We can see

For free.

Sun Dreams
(A faerie's point of view)

If someday, or night,
I dream of true light,
If one night I dream of the sun,

In which does not exist,

Then I know I've experienced life.

As if silver dragons and golden rabbits

ever satisfied my eyes.

Humans are in all the human tales

The way they live is absolutely amazing!

They have hornless unicorns

And furry dragons without wings that do not breathe fire.

Dreams

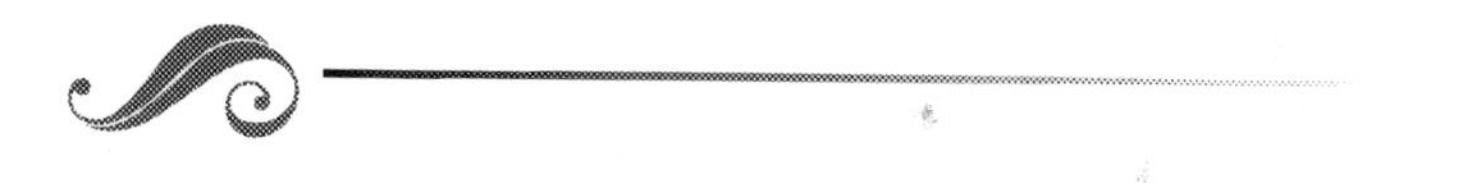

What is a dream?

Can you find it?

Do you have to travel the universe for it?

Or does it come to you?

Is it a gift from God?

And when you have it, what do you do with it?

Do you keep it in a jar?

Do you place it in a locket, and carry

it with you everywhere?

Do you hold it in your hands and whisper a wish to it?

Or does it not exist?

If it does, I will keep it safe in my heart

Pray To the Stars

Even in the day I look to the sky
I close my eyes and say my thoughts to myself.
If they are clever enough, I write
them down for safe keeping.

So, one day if someone is to be my friend and listen,

That will be the day I no longer need to write.

When I don't write, I pray to the stars.

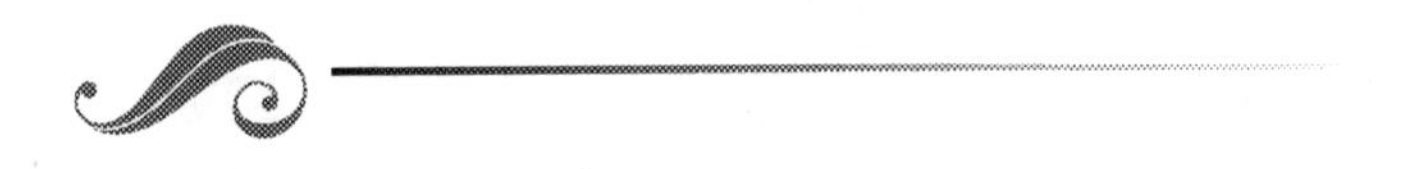

Warning: Fragile

So you found out that your heart is made of glass.

Cracked and chipped from the ones you loved before.

Your skin is paper.

Torn and wrinkled by your past experiences.

Every word you've said tattooed between each line,
connecting each freckle like a constellation.
Now that you've realized how fragile you are, try this.
Instead of trying to glue your warm paper palm to others,

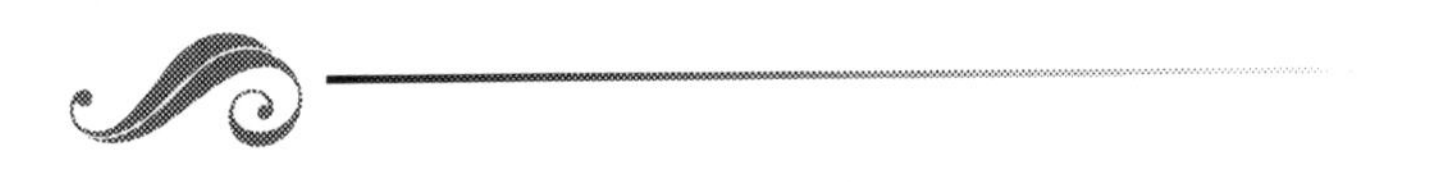

Begging them to notice you,

To forgive you,

By tearing off pieces of you to patch up their experiences,

Try fixing your own tears and iron your wrinkles.

Tape back on the pieces of you that you forgot matter.

So your bones are glass

And your flesh is paper.

Only you treat yourself this way,

Your bones are charged crystal

And your paper is tough skin.

So move on. You're more important than

the one thing holding you back.

Love

I Am A Free Bird

I set myself free from the cage that once kept me hostage

And have been hurt

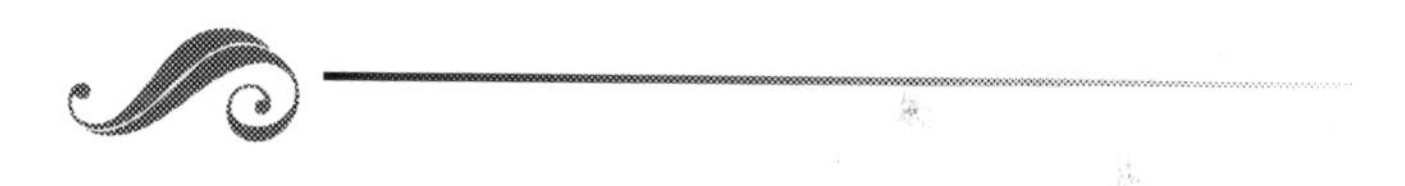

And under the advantage of another

I am a free bird once again!

But they might still be hunting me...

A Breath

Every breath I take
Feels like the inhale
Is filling my lungs with water.

Every exhale
Is alcohol on a cut.
Breathing hurts now that you've gone for good.

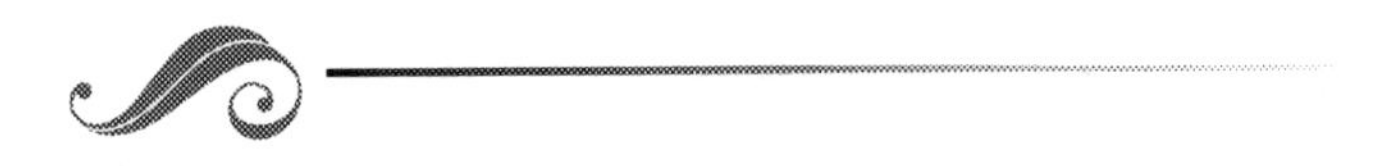

Though, then again...

It's been such a pain since I've fallen

When I Fell

Love isn't supposed to hurt

But it did.

When I fell in love, no one was there to catch me.

When I fell, I landed on my heart.

It hurt.

And where was he to catch me when I fell?

Printed in the United States
By Bookmasters